WATER GARDEN CONSTRUCTION

A Technical Guide for Designers

Martin Kelley

PACKARD PUBLISHING LIMITED

CHICHESTER

WATER GARDEN CONSTRUCTION

A Technical Guide for Designers

© Martin Kelley

First published in 2015 by Packard Publishing Limited, 14 Guilden Road, Chichester, West Sussex, PO19 7LA, UK.

All rights reserved. No part of this book may be reproduced or transmitted in any form or by any means, electronic or mechanical including recording, or by any information storage and retrieval system, without the written permission of the publisher. Restricted photocopying is permitted under licence from the Copyright Licensing Agency, London, or its international equivalents.

Cover photo by Fairwater Ltd. Designer: Nigel Philips.

ISBN 978 185341 150 2

Commissioned, edited and prepared for press by Michael Packard.

Designed and laid out by Hilite Design and Reprographics Limited, Marchwood, Southampton, Hampshire.

Printed and bound in the United Kingdom by PublishPoint, KnowledgePoint Limited, Winnersh, Wokingham, Berkshire.

Acknowledgements

All photographs, line drawings and plans are by the Author or his company, Fairwater Ltd, unless otherwise acknowledged. The work of the following garden and landscape designers, architects and landscapers is gratefully acknowledged:

Acres Wild, Artscape, Marcus Barnett, Janet Bligh, Lara Copley-Smith, Luciano Giubbilei, Greenprint Garden Design, Richard Key, Martin Lane-Fox, Fiona Lawrenson, Rose Lennard, Tim Lynch, John Murdoch, Kevin Murphy, Nigel Philips, Elizabeth Ramsay, Julie Toll, Andrew Wilson; Bell Fischer Architects, Berkeley Homes, The Garden Company, Guncast Swimming Pools Ltd, Landmark Ltd, London Wildlife Trust.

Lake and waterfall. Photo: Fairwater. Designer: Rose Lennard.

CONTENTS

Introduction	iv
PART 1 FORMAL WATER GARDENS	**1**
Formal water gardens	1
Some basic construction details	1
Pool liners	2
CASE STUDY: Raised rectangular pond with jets	**3**
Bill of quantities	7
Examples of water courses in formal settings	7
Infinity edges	9
Alternatives to chemicals	10
Water pavements	11
Jumping jets	11
CASE STUDY: Brimming pools	**11**
Bill of quantities	13
Water tables	14
Water pumps	15
Flow rates	16
Water garden safety	17
Water walls	19
Water usage	21
Chutes	22
Errors in construction	23
Summary	23
PART 2 INFORMAL WATER GARDENS	**24**
Informality in the garden	24
Excavation	25
Definition of lakes and ponds	26
Liners for lakes and ponds	27
Clay	27
Bentonite	27
Concrete	28
Fibreglass	28
Flexible sheet materials	28
Butyl and EPDM	29
Butyl or Greenseal EPDM	29
Beneath the liner	30
The fringes of ponds and lakes	31
Marginal planting	32
Clay-lined ponds	33
CASE STUDY: Extending a clay-lined pond	**35**
Bill of quantities	37
Natural water courses	38
Topography	39
Waterfalls and streams	40
Types of stone	40
Construction	41
Examples of the effective use of water	42
Water storage and attenuation	43
The maturing pond	44
Summary	45
Further Reading	**45**
Index	**46**

FIGURES

Typical section of pool lining	2
Raised rectangular pool — plan and section for Winchester garden	3
Balancing tank	6
Plan and section for two parallel water pavements	12
Pumping calculation	15
Water usage	21
Bentonite installation	27
Section through groundwater 'vent' arrangement	30
Detail of pond-edge construction	32
Detail of pond-edge planting	32
Details of a clay-lined pond construction	34
Detail of timber rail installation	36
Typical section through a constructed waterfall	38

Water feature. Designer: Kevin Murphy.

INTRODUCTION

Twenty-five years ago I had the privilege of meeting Anthony Archer-Wills and working with him for the following 10 years in his water-garden construction business. Anthony's innovations in construction techniques are still used throughout the industry and many are described in his first book, *The Water Gardener* published by Frances Lincoln, which I still recommend as a reference for anyone interested in water-garden construction.

This book is based on my experience of working with Anthony, and subsequently with my own company, Fairwater Limited. Later I was asked to lecture on water gardens and landscapes to the students at the Oxford College of Garden Design and other institutions. The pages that follow in this book, therefore, reflect my lectures to those students and the answers to many of their questions.

I describe some of the processes and techniques we use in the technical design and construction of water gardens. I cover characteristics of formal water gardens – ponds, rills, canals, fountains, weirs and water walls – and then move on to informal pools, lakes, waterfalls and streams.

Water-garden construction, as with all landscape, falls into two main categories. The first is concerned with formal features, such as geometrically shaped pools using hard-landscape materials to provide walls, copings and so on, which are usually located in the formal parts of the garden nearest the house. The second category focuses on the informal water garden where we attempt to mimic the natural world by creating wildlife ponds, lakes, streams and waterfalls that appear to have formed naturally.

Martin Kelley

'Natural' lake outside Henley.
Designer: Martin Lane-Fox.

Mirror pond with stepping stones in Hampshire.
Designer: Rose Lennard.

Glacial boulder stream in Surrey.
Designer: Elizabeth Ramsay.

PART 1 FORMAL WATER GARDENS

Formal water gardens

Any water garden will only be deemed a success if it fulfils two essential objectives: first, it retains water, and secondly that the water remains clean and healthy. Get these wrong, and the pond will soon become the most depressing part of the garden. Get them right, and the water garden will become the heart of the garden, where there will be a sense of movement and vitality as light dances on the water surface on a cold winter's morning, or dragonflies and iris display their gaudy colours in early summer.

Stepped canal. Designer: Marcus Barnett.

Some basic construction details

A formal pool will, by its nature, have rigid sides to define its shape, normally constructed from brick, concrete block, poured concrete, stone or even timber. These walls have to be constructed as if they are garden retaining-walls, for the dry land beyond the pool is heavier than the water within it, and an inward pressure is therefore exerted on the structures.

In order to prevent the walls moving and cracking, it is usual practice to include a vertical expansion joint in the wall every 2m or so. This, however, gives us a water-proofing problem, as any render or paint applied across these joints will also crack. The retaining walls, therefore, need to be engineered to such a high standard that they cannot crack – at vast expense with reinforced concrete – or designed to be flexible.

A further complication to the design of the pool's retaining walls is that they will on occasion need to accommodate sudden changes in shape, such as boxed-out segments in the rill above, or that the pool may be raised above the ground such as this roundabout pool (right).

In this example the pool is approximately 450mm above the surrounding drive. This height works well when preventing cars falling into the pond.

*Raised 'roundabout' pool.
Designer: Luciano Giubbilei.*

Rill with box sections. Designer: Rose Lennard.

When constructing these simple formal pools in a domestic garden, a cost-effective solution is to incorporate a flexible sheet liner within a cavity wall structure. This process overcomes the problem of slight wall movement, because a good quality rubber liner will be at least 200 per cent elastic, easily accommodating a hair line crack in a wall.

Finished rill and planting. Designer: Artscape.

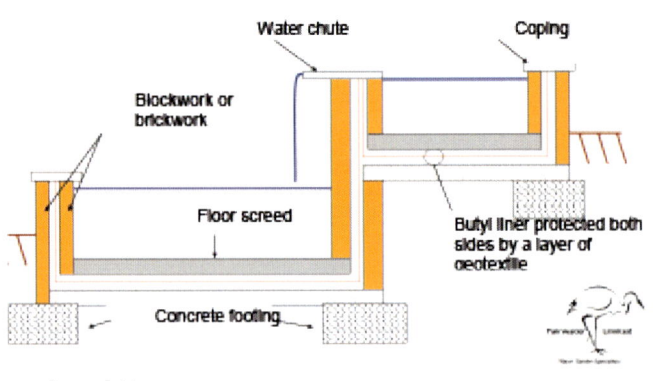

Rill during construction. Designer: Artscape.

Pond liners

The picture above shows a rectangular pool under construction, and you can see the black lining-material between the two walls of the pool. The outer wall will have face work, in this case yellow London stock bricks, and the internal wall is a cheap, dense, aggregate concrete block. The floor of the pond has been screeded over to protect the liner.

Once completed the liners are entirely hidden from view and protected by the masonry, as shown above. This technique of sandwiching liners between masonry is extremely flexible and allows builders or landscapers to construct ponds with no specialist skills.

If you look at a generic construction drawing, you can see how the water is retained within a bag of pond liner which is, in turn, encased in masonry.

The footings and wall sizes will depend on the size of the finished pool, ground conditions and so on. They should be finally sanctioned by the site engineer. A rule of thumb, however, is that the twin 100mm-wide wall shown is suitable for walls of up to 600mm; any higher and they will need to be thicker, certainly at the bottom.

An alternative method of construction is to build a solid concrete box, and then fit a structural fibre-glass skin to the inside.

The fibre-glass acts as an inner skin and is supported by the concrete behind. This is technically more advanced than the liner option, and is generally used in commercial projects. The colour of the fibre-glass can be varied but is typically black.

CASE STUDY – Raised rectangular pond with jets

This is a project we were involved in a few years ago, and should serve to demonstrate both the design and the construction process.

At the request of a garden designer, I attended a meeting on site within the shadow of Winchester Cathedral. The proposal was to create a small, raised, rectangular pool in the apex of a triangular garden in front of a new pergola hiding a shed.

This is the site plan showing these elements.

To begin with, there was a three-way discussion between the client, designer and

Fibre-glass being applied to a concrete shell, London. Photo: Fairwater.

Fibre-glass lined pond awaiting copings, Central London. Designer: Bell Fischer Architects.

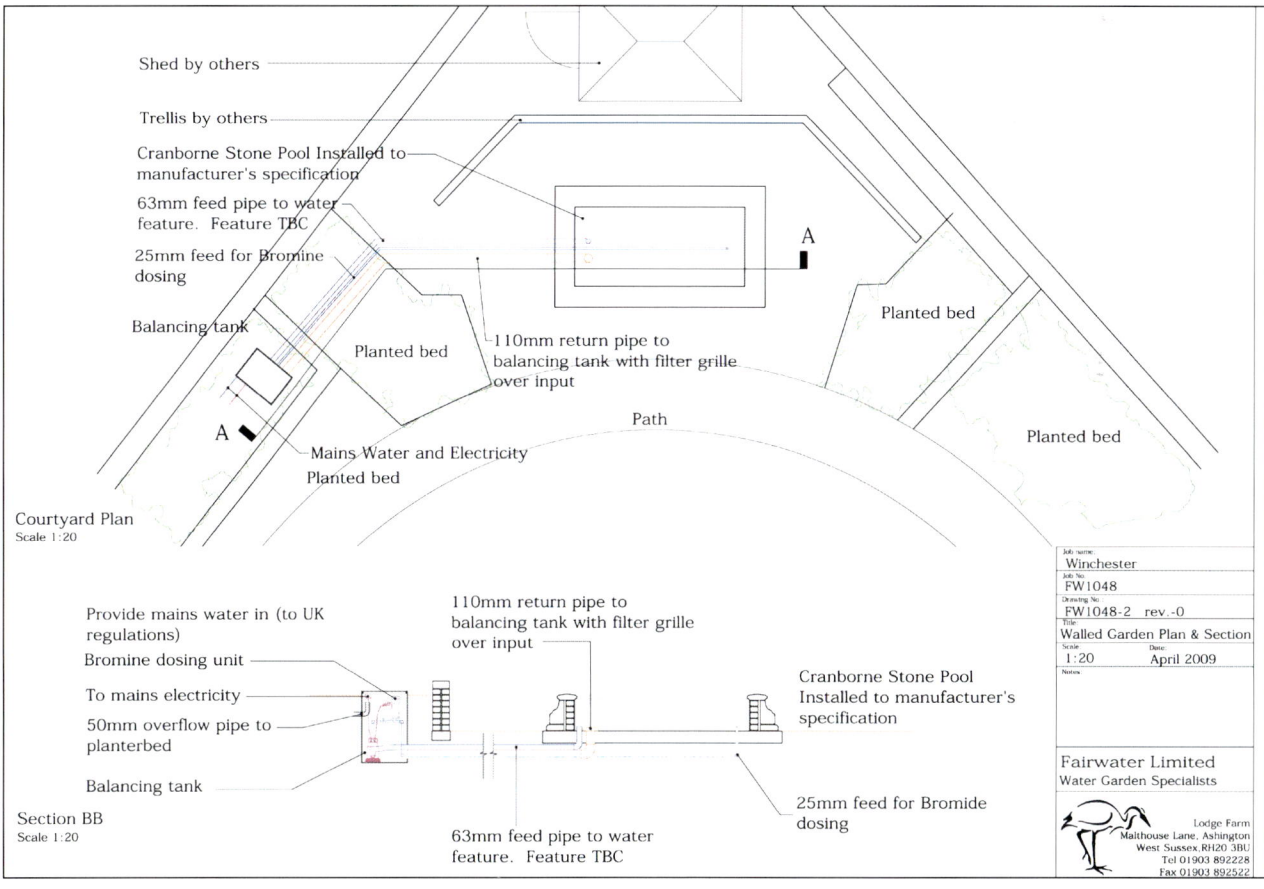

Greenprint's design for the Winchester garden.

Clients' illustrative photos.

myself. All of us had different ideas as to what would be the most suitable fountain display and pool design in this area. I was particularly concerned that we could end up with something the client did not like. I suggested that they emailed me some pictures to illustrate their preferred options.

You can see from the pictures they sent (above) that we were wildly adrift from each other as these two displays are totally inappropriate for the site in Winchester!

I estimated that the fountains in the Canadian gorge were 20 to 30m high, which would require a pool diameter of around 50m to ensure that most of the water is caught as it falls back. As a general rule, the fountain-jet height should not exceed the radius of the pool receiving the water.

The second picture shows a typical corporate fountain ring or crown; again far too large and municipal for our small raised pond in Winchester.

On occasions when a design team and client's ideas are so far apart, I find it advisable to 'mock up' the water garden if at all possible. I was concerned that the client was going to be disappointed with the rather more modest display I proposed if they had not seen it as a full-scale model. Of equal concern, there was the risk of water loss and the noise of the feature. So the construction of a model of the pool enabled all these issues to be considered by client and designer before significant sums were spent on site.

Water-garden mock-up in Fairwater's yard.

By using old sleepers, an off-cut of pond liner and a section of the proposed pool surround, we created a functional, if not exact, replica of the pool destined for the client's garden.

We moved on to the construction, having finally agreed the design. The next picture shows the faux-Portland stone surround placed on top of the 300mm-deep, reinforced-concrete foundation slab. The stone is taking the place of the face brickwork in the earlier example of the liner sandwich construction.

diameter pipe, called the balancing pipe, a smaller 50mm-diameter pipe which will feed the fountains, and a second feed pipe of 32mm which will operate the water-cleansing circuit.

Passing a pipe through the liner means it can be easily hidden in a floor screed or brought in below water. It is essential, however, that the liner penetration is done with care using suitable fittings such as the mechanical flange shown here. The liner is clamped between the two plates and secured with stainless steel bolts.

The larger of the two return pipes, the 50mm-diameter one, has been extended to form the ladder-like structure you can see on the pond floor. The purpose of this is to ensure the water pressure within the pipe-work is equal, and the three fountain jets will all attain the same height. If these jets were simply fed three in a row, the first would receive more water than the last, and the jet heights would vary accordingly.

Portland-stone pond under construction, Winchester. Photo: Fairwater.

Typical pipe-flange assembly for passing through liners. Photo: Fairwater.

Portland-stone pond under construction, Winchester. Photo: Fairwater.

You can see the grey geotextile membrane being used to protect the liner from both above and below, and you can see three pipes passing through the liner. These are a large 160mm-

The pool's construction has now progressed with the liners encased by the internal wall of brick and concrete block.

The smaller, 32mm return pipe can be seen in the top corner; this is bringing clean water to the pool.

Portland-stone pool under construction, Winchester. Photo: Greenprint.

Balancing-tank housing top-up, overflow, pumps and dosing unit, Winchester. Photo: Fairwater.

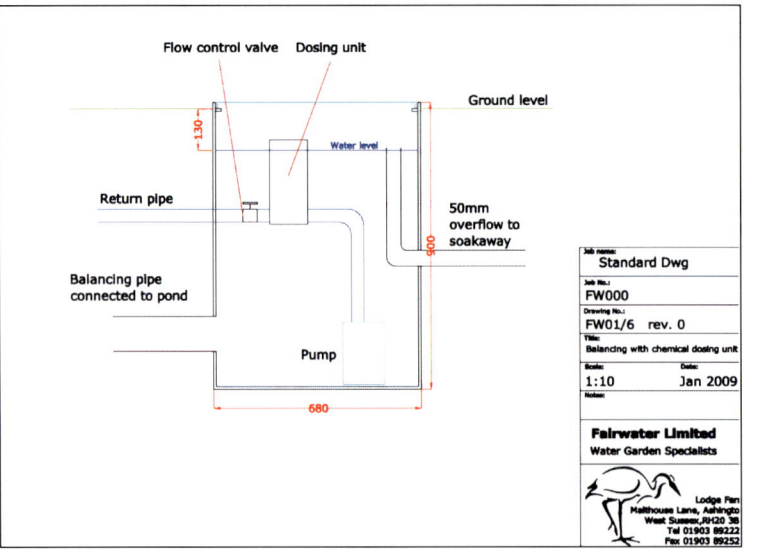

We are nearing completion. The pipes in the pool floor have been screeded over and the three jets are being trialled. You will have noted the three pipes leaving the pool in a trench. These pipes are connected to an external tank known as the balancing tank. This tank is housed in the raised border near to the pond and shares the same water level as the pond; the two bodies of water are connected below the water line by the large-bore, 160mm-diameter balancing pipe.

The water level of the pond can be controlled remotely by means of a mains water supply on a float valve and a concealed overflow. The tank also provides a home for the chemical dosing unit which will prevent the water turning green, and the two pumps – one to operate the fountains and the other for the dosing.

Two pumps are used to allow the fountains to be switched off independently of the filtration, thereby ensuring the water remains clean when the clients are away.

The section above shows the balancing tank. The tank is manufactured from 12mm polypropylene. It has the same footprint as a standard manhole cover, namely 450mm by 600mm, and is typically 90mm deep. It must be sited in such a way as to ensure the pond water level is around 150mm below the rim to ensure there is dry space to house the top-up valve and electrical junction boxes.

6 FORMAL WATER GARDENS

Water treatment

The dosing unit contains slow-dissolving chlorine or bromine tablets. Both will ensure the water is clear of pathogens and will prevent the growth of algae. Algae, being the simplest form of life in a pond, are the foundation of the food chain. If the algae cannot grow, a pond ecosystem will not develop and the water will remain clear. Chlorine is cheaper and more efficient than bromine but has the distinctive smell. We tend to use bromine in domestic gardens and chlorine in commercial installations where ongoing cost outweighs the inconvenience of smell.

Untreated pond water is classified by the WRAS as category 5 waste as it may contain pathogens such as Wiles disease and *cryptosporidium*. As a result any mains water top-up must be supplied to the pond via a break gap set at least 300mm above ground level. This will ensure that pond water cannot possibly back-siphon into the domestic water supply. This air gap is typically achieved by feeding the pond from a header tank in an adjacent building or mounted on a wall.

Even chemically-treated pond water, as in this case, is classed as category 5 waste as it is reliant on human intervention to maintain the chemical dosing.

Here is another example of the wall-and-liner sandwich being used in this garden at a retirement complex in Surrey.

Raised pool and rill. Designer: Tim Lynch.

Rill and raised pond seen from the opposite direction. Designer: Tim Lynch.

The raised pool is of rendered and painted block work, and is set above the ground to provide good access for wheelchairs.

The copper feature is an off-the-shelf cup device available from Stowasis – their website offers all manner of simple, inexpensive features to add to formal pools.

The pool overflows into a rill crossing the lawn. This rill is also constructed from a block wall encased in pond liner, and is covered in toughened glass where it crosses the paving.

Covering a water feature in glass is always problematic and often results in condensation forming on the underside as a result of the difference in temperature between the air above and the water below.

The rill ends in the circular sump containing the trellis pole. This is a good example of the importance of using a balancing tank, as the reservoir would be too small and inaccessible to house the recirculation and dosing equipment.

Cobbled rill. Photo: Berkeley Homes.

Formal water garden. Designer: Janet Bligh.

The picture above shows another rill or narrow canal which has been edged and faced in flamed granite with cobbles set in the floor. I generally advise against using cobbles and shingles on pool floors as they act as a pre-filter, collecting debris and silt. Loose shingle is very difficult to clean and will get sucked in by vacuum equipment. White shingle is particularly difficult as it is prone to turning green when algae colonize it. The chlorine or bromine in the water will soon dissipate on contact with the air, which is why the dosing is constant and both chemicals only treat the water, not structures, the floor or walls; these will require occasional scrubbing to remove filamentous algae such as blanket weed.

These stones have been mortared down to accommodate cleaning by vacuum, and to prevent them from being used as missiles in this public space.

A further example of the flexibility offered by the liner and masonry technique is shown above with a raised pool feeding a narrow stone rill which drops into a sunken pool. The use of the liner has allowed the beautiful face stonework to be continued down into the water.

If a simple, black rendered surface is all that is required within the pool and the substructure and footings are sufficient, alternatives to the liner system described so far would be to cover the internal walls with a waterproof render such as SIKA, or to apply a waterproof coat to a standard render. The latter could be the cheaper budgetary option, which is proprietary pond paint such as G4, the more durable GRP or fibreglass. All these materials will be at risk of damage by being on the face of the walls, and none has much flexibility, should the wall move.

Infinity edges

The pool (lower left) is again constructed from block-work and liners, but here is clad in Kirkstone green slate. The water, rather than lapping the bottom of the coping, is constantly flowing over the edge into a collection gully around the pool. This type of feature is termed an 'infinity edge'. It will always give a brimming pool, as the water level is set by an enlarged balancing-tank acting as the below-ground reservoir.

The water is pumped from the reservoir into the pond floor where it is baffled to prevent surface ripples, and so provide the mirror-calm finish.

To maintain the crystal-clear water, bromine is added via a chemical dosing unit in the balancing-tank. As we have seen, bromine, similar to chlorine, prevents the single-celled algae from colonizing the water and also kills pathogens. It has to be constantly added via slow-dissolving tablets, as the chemical dissipates rapidly on contact with the air.

Infinity-edge pool. Photo: Fairwater.

The infinity edge can be improved by replacing the wide coping stone with a 10mm knife edge of copper or steel. The stunning example overlooking the Surrey Hills (top right) has a copper lip clamped to the pond lining, and really does give the impression of water connecting to the horizon.

As is the case with the other pools in this section, this pond is dosed with bromine, and there is no other form of filtration included. To remove all debris, floating leaves, grass cuttings, silt and detritus from a pond, will require the installation of swimming-pool quality mechanical filtration. This will include surface skimmers, bottom drains and large external sand filters. I regard this as excessive for an ornamental water garden, and its cost is generally prohibitive.

Infinity-edge pool. Designer: Fiona Lawrenson.

I advise my clients to drain and clean their pools every year or two to limit the accumulation of silt, and either enjoy watching leaves on the water surface or scoop them off with a net each morning!

Returning to the construction detail, a close-up of the weir during maintenance (below) shows the copper angle knife-edge sitting on the black, rendered block-wall.

Alternatives to chemicals

We have so far touched on adding chemicals to the water to prevent algal growth which is responsible for turning water green. The pool shown below is an example of an alternative solution when chemicals are not part of the client brief.

Rather than add an external, bulky and unsightly filter to the pond, in this garden we have turned the lower pool into an under-gravel filter. Perforated pipes are connected to the balancing pipe and then buried in shingle. This ensures that any water reaching the balancing tank has had to pass through the shingle, and is therefore mechanically filtered.

The addition of marginal plants, in this case *Iris laevigata*, planted directly into the gravel helps combat algae growth. The absence of soil means that the iris must find their nutrients from the water itself and in so doing compete with the algae for their food source. I shall describe this process in more detail later on pages 32 and 33. Algae-eating bacteria will naturally thrive in the top layer of the shingle which will further aid the process.

The formal pools described so far will have a typical depth of 600mm of water. Pools relying on the naturally balanced ecosystem, or a biological filter to keep them clean, will require a depth of water to restrict algal growth by maintaining a stable temperature.

Close-up of an Infinity-edge pool. Photo: Fairwater.

Formal pool with plants. Photo: Landmark.

Water pavements

Water pavement. Photo: Landmark.

If a pool is chemically treated, however, a very thin film of water can be created. The example here of a water pavement in North London is a steel tray set over a block-and-liner reservoir in-filled with granite slabs. The water is pumped from a balancing tank into the tray where it wells up through the un-mortared joints to spread out at about 5mm depth before dropping over the perimeter edge. The white residue on the stones is limescale from the mains water. This can be treated by adding swimming pool acid to the system or by fitting a water softener, provided that there is a suitable housing available. The holes in the slabs are for a 'jumping jet'.

Jumping jets

Jumping jets or Laminar flow jets are extremely precise plumes of water that maintain their shape as they fly through the air. The units that generate them are complex machines controlled by steptronic motors. They are capable of controlling the flow to such an extent that they can be set to music, or cause the jet to stop and start so rapidly that the fountain plume appears to have been cut into small sections of water.

The jets are expensive owing to their complexity, but a domestic range is available for around £2500.00.

CASE STUDY – Brimming pools

Another example of the water pavement is the steel version shown below. A pair of tables either side of a staircase were constructed on a site in Surrey from powder-coated black stainless steel sheet housed on a box section frame located within a prefabricated polypropylene tank.

The plan on the following page shows how the two pavements are linked to a common balancing tank in the border.

Steel-water pavement showing the polypropylene reservoir connected to the large-diameter balancing pipe, the green delivery hose and the box steel frame ready to support the pavement. Designer: Andrew Wilson.

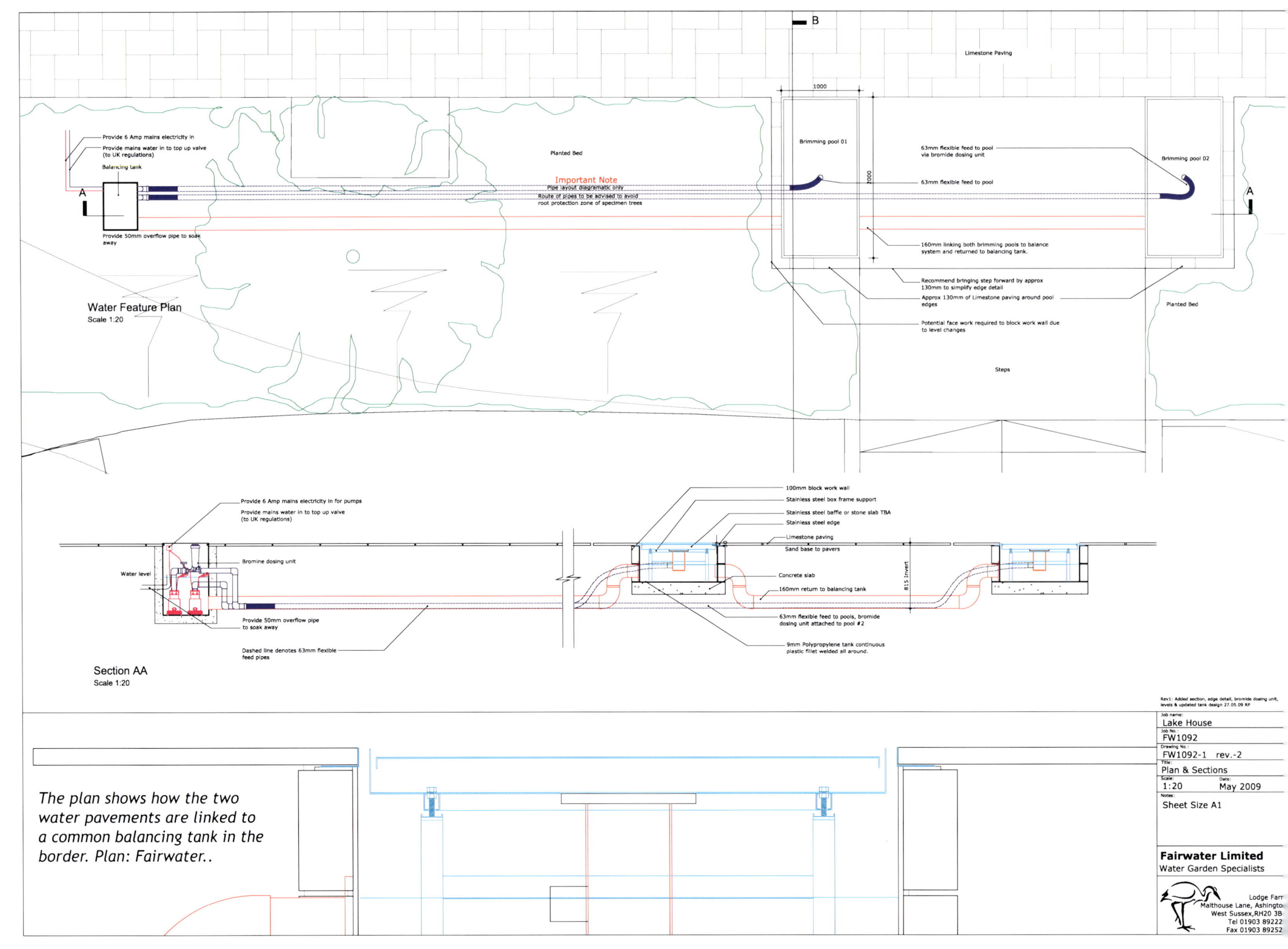

Finally the two pavements are set level in the paving and the balancing tank is lost in the planting in the foreground.

The steel water pavements during construction. Photo: Fairwater. Designer: Andrew Wilson.

Bill of Quantities

Job: Brimming Pools
Designed by Andrew wilson
Budget Costs Jan 2015
All figures are subject to the addition of VAT

Code	Description	Quantity	Unit	Rate	Total
A	TECHNICAL DESIGN To complete working construction drawings for features	1.00	sum	2,185.50	2,185.50
B	EXCAVATIONS Excavate for pools and tank, cart all surplus spoil off site	1.00	sum	697.00	697.00
C	FOOTINGS Pour concrete slabs to accommodate pools	1.00	sum	658.50	658.50
D	BLOCK WALLS 110mm solid concrete block walls to form pool surrounds; nominal 600mm deep,	1.00	sum	1,472.70	1,472.70
E	LINING Supply and fit pre formed polypropelene tanks to form reservoirs for pools	2.00	each	1,192.50	2,385.00
F	BRIMMING POOL MECHANISM Manufacture steel rims, support mechanism, base tray etc. to create brimming pools Powder coat in colour to be confirmed Fit to tanks on site	2.00	each	2,910.00	5,820.00
G	BALANCING TANK Supply and fit a single 450mm x 600mm x 900mm deep balancing tank in border Connect to the two reservoirs via large bore pipes	1.00	each	2,161.70	2,161.70
I	COPING Haunch tanks with concrete as required. Fit coping to new walls at rear of pools	1.00	sum	2,130.00	2,130.00
J	COMMISSIONING Fill pools and set all levels Connect service tails supplied to tank position by others Install recirculation pumps, mains water top up, overflow and chemical dosing unit Hand over c/w instruction handbook	1.00	sum	1,970.09	1,970.09
	TOTAL				£19,480.49

Water tables

The concept of a thin film of water can be applied to raised structures. In the example below, the water is spreading across a water table and dropping into a surrounding pool, itself raised to 450mm above ground with a wide coping for sitting on.

The original design required a sheet of water falling from the edge of the raised section. This would have been very noisy, and it would have been impossible to force enough water to produce this effect through the central hole without creating a fountain.

The slower flow of water resulted in a broken stream of water around the table which produced a gentle sound suitable for this entertainment space.

A variation on the water table theme is the circular example. This has been designed for the inner pool delivering the water to act as a wine cooler and, once again, the falling water is in broken streams rather than a constant sheet to ensure a pleasant, not invasive sound.

Raised water table. Designer: Fiona Lawrenson.

Close-up of the raised water table. Designer: Fiona Lawrenson.

Circular water table. Designer Lara Copley-Smith.

Water pumps

The majority of modern water garden installations will require the installation of pumps to provide the moving water. Naturally flowing water may be available in a few cases, but generally pumps are employed in the formal features described so far.

Pumping water is a vast subject, but an overview will give a basic understanding of the terminology.

There are two pieces of information required to specify a pump. These are the flow-rate or speed at which the water is being delivered; always described as a volume of water per unit of time, expressed most commonly in litres per minute. The second value required is termed the 'head', which is the vertical distance the water is being lifted from the water level in the reservoir to the point of discharge. These values are shown on a graph which shows the higher the water is being lifted, the slower it will flow.

The pump should be specified at a mid-point on its graph.

Two types of pump are commonly used; submersible and surface.

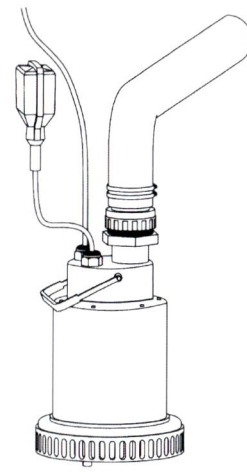

The submersible pump is most commonly used as it is simple to install; the whole unit is placed in the water and connected to the delivery hose.

The advantage of this type of pump is that it will not be susceptible to frost damage in the winter, and it does not require priming – the process whereby air is removed from the inlet to allow the unit to suck.

Submersible pumps cannot be used in swimming pools as they require mains voltage electricity which could liven the water should a fault occur.

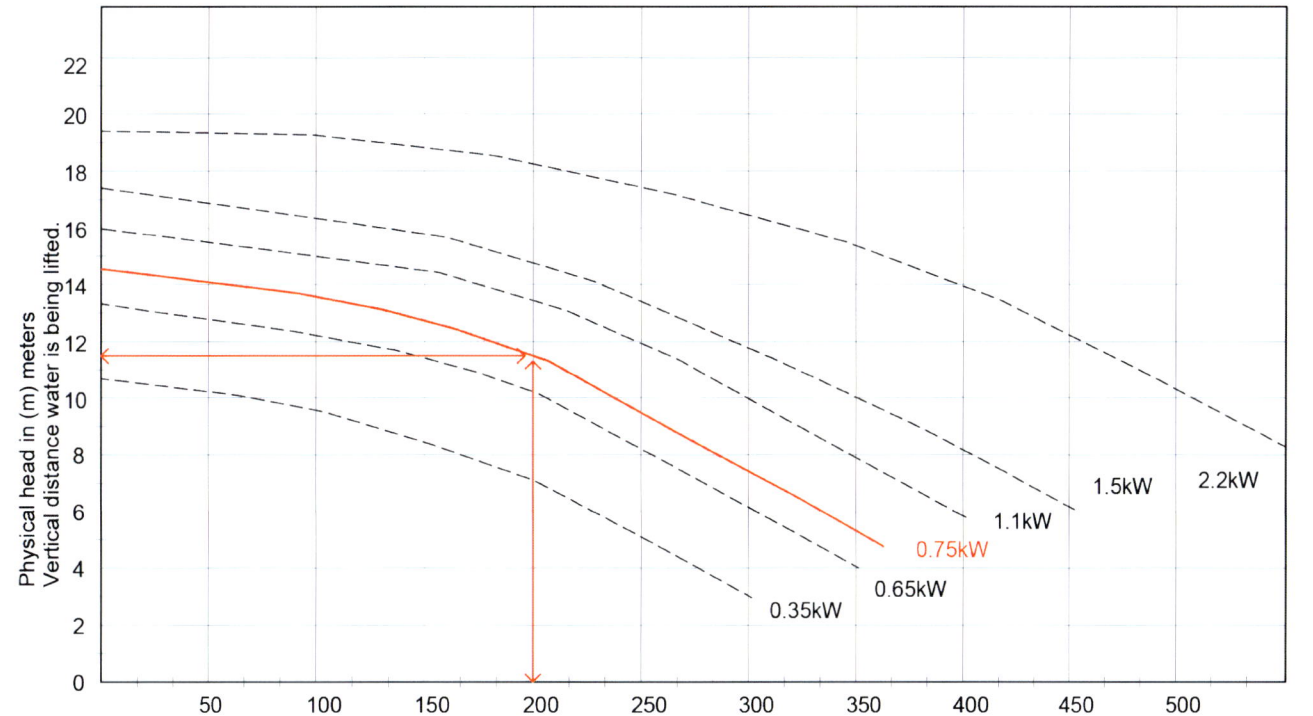

PUMP CALCULATION

Surface pump. Photo: Fairwater.

The alternative to a submersible pump is *a surface pump*. These are housed in a shed or dry chamber outside the pond and draw water through a suction line. Surface pumps tend to generate more pressure than submersibles and are sometimes used for fountain displays or for installations where the pool is designed for people to enter. The electric motor must be kept away from the water.

As they are not being protected by a depth of water, these pumps must be drained down in the winter to prevent damage from frosting. They will only work once they have been primed, or the air has been removed from the suction line.

Flow rates

A garden hose with good pressure will generate about 10 litres per minute, which equates to approximately 600 litres per hour.

From my calculations over the years, a clear sheet of water will be achieved when water is passed over a spillway at a rate faster than 40 litres per minute per 300mm width. Less than this rate will result in a broken water pattern.

KEY: l/m = litres per minute
m3h = cubic metres per hour
l/s = litres per second

Examples:
1 tap flows at 650 to 1000 l/h or 1m3/h or c.10 l/m (c. 220 gallons per hour)

>40 l/m per 300mm width.

<40 l/m per 300mm width.

Water garden safety

Pond safety grilles. Photo: Fairwater.

The Serpentine, Hyde Park, London. Photo: Fairwater.

This is an emotive subject and one that will come up in discussions with clients during the design process.

When my son was born I had a raised brick pool in my garden and my wife was concerned that we should ensure our new child could not get into the water. I argued that being raised, the child would have to be at least three years old before he would be able to get into the water, by which time he would understand that it was cold and unpleasant and have no desire to get in. My wife was not of that opinion and so I commissioned this rather municipal-looking grille and fitted it to the pond.

Although this is a rather unsightly solution, it does illustrate two important points when placing a grille over a pond. First, the grille is strong enough to be walked on and, second, it is above the water so a small face cannot make contact with the water should the child fall over.

Drowning

When considering water safety, it is important to understand some other statistics. Drowning is rare in the UK with on average only 430 people per year drowning in the sea, rivers, lakes and at home. Of these about ten per cent will be children under 14. Fifteen per cent of child drownings occur in the bath, and it is only one or two who drown in garden ponds or swimming pools; the majority are claimed by the sea or fast-flowing rivers.

Putting drowning into perspective, however, does not remove the fact that any drowning is a disaster and steps must be taken to prevent it from happening.

More details of drowning statistics can be found on the ROSPA website.

Ponds

The rules for public water safety are generally vague and vary between local authorities. The picture of the Serpentine in London's Hyde Park shows an unfenced path running into the water with nothing but a warning sign and life ring to mitigate the risk.

Submerged safety grid. Photo: Fairwater.

Bespoke pond grille. Designer: Robin Templar Williams.

Pond at 10 Downing Street. Designer: Julie Toll.

Some authorities require park lakes to have deep water at the margin to allow people to fall in without hitting structures. Others insist on shallow margins to allow people to walk in and out. I think that the latter is safer.

There are some proprietary systems available such as the 'safa' **pond grid system**. This is a series of interlocking tables placed into the water that provide a safety grille normally 50mm below water level. I find this expensive to install, and do not like the fact it is 50mm below water: a child could fall face first into the water and still drown.

An alternative to the submerged grille is one placed above the water. This could be part of the design with water-lily motifs and ornamental metal work as in the example (left).

In 2000 we were commissioned by the London Wildlife Trust to build a pond in the quietest of the Royal Parks, the back garden of number 10 Downing Street.

On completion the pond was to be 'launched' by the BBC children's programme 'Blue Peter', and the No. 10 press office was looking forward to some good PR over the summer. Sadly, however, there was a terrible accident in a Sussex village when a two-year-old left his carer, went next door and fell into a farm pond where he drowned. As the Prime Minister's wife was pregnant at the time and, coupled with a campaign launched by the

Bubbling rocks. Designer Lara Copley-Smith.

Daily Mirror newspaper against garden ponds, the press office called a meeting of all health and safety professionals to consider the safety of this new pond. After a long debate it was concluded that there is no such thing as a safe pond, and the only way to protect people from open water is to fence it off. This is what was then done and a suitable press release was issued.

If safety is a concern, there are plenty of options to enjoy water gardens without having open water. The reservoirs can be concealed below ground and fountains, sculptures, water walls or drilled boulders employed to run the water over.

Such installations benefit from the addition of a balancing tank since the concealed reservoir will make access to the pump difficult. These features also use significant quantities of water, as the fine film of water moving across a smooth surface will be susceptible to evaporation. This water loss will not be visible and an automated top-up is advisable.

Glass water wall: Designer The Garden Company.

Water walls

These provide a convenient method of producing vertical water features without having to move the water too quickly. The sound of water falling for several metres is often intrusive and can result in severe splashing; running it down a water wall will give an interesting effect at low flow rates of about 10 l/m per 300mm width, rather than the 40 needed to produce a clean free-falling chute.

The water can be run down many materials including glass, stone, steel or copper and, provided the surface is smooth, the water will form wave-like patterns.

The glass example here is fed by a spray bar at the top which results in the quite definite lines.

The water is treated with bromine to prevent algal growth and is re-circulated via a balancing tank and submersible pump.

A variation on the water-wall theme is to combine the wall with water pavements to create raised plinths such as this example.

A lined block structure (right) has been clad in granite and fitted with a steel tray on top. The tray is filled with loosely laid granite slabs, and the pumped water wells up through the un-mortared joints before spreading out

Granite water plinth: Designer: Berkeley Homes.

as a 5mm-deep film and dropping over the vertical sides. A collection channel carries the water to a balancing tank beneath the recessed manhole covers seen in the surrounding paving.

Water walls can be constructed on a large scale. The group of stainless steel towers (next page) in the left-hand picture range from 4.5m high down to 2.5m. They were fabricated from polished stainless steel which, although a giving a dramatic effect, did present maintenance problems as the lime-scale and the dust that blew across the site were extremely visible and difficult to combat with filtration.

Stainless-steel water towers.
Designer: Berkeley Homes.

Brushed stainless-steel water towers.
Designer: Berkeley Homes.

Granite water tower.
Designer: Berkeley Homes.

Rather than polished, a brushed stainless steel can be used to offset these problems as in the above middle picture.

A further example of a 4m-high water wall is the granite-clad structure (right). Even though this is of a considerable size, the water can all be collected in a narrow, 75mm-wide channel in the paving: the surface tension of the water causes it to cling to the smooth stone face, only splashing as a result of strong gusts of wind.

A further variation on the water wall is the Chadar. This is originally an Islamic feature, the word meaning sheet or shawl, and was originally used as a means of conveying irrigation water from a high level. Whereas a smooth water wall would never be more than five degrees from the vertical to allow the water to spread evenly across the face, a Chadar would typically lean back by 15 degrees and would have a textured face.

*Chadar water wall.
Designer: The Garden Company.*

The texture causes white water and increases evaporation, possibly to encourage cooling of the air as these structures were installed within warm courtyards.

Water usage

All of the above features will use significant quantities of water because a thin film of moving water is readily absorbed by the atmosphere. It is impossible to quantify the rate of water-loss from any feature by evaporation as this process is dependent on many external factors. These would include air temperature, relative humidity, wind speed and direction, the water temperature, and so on.

The graph here demonstrates the increase in evaporation when water is moved. A series of identical tanks was placed in a sunny position and filled to the same level with water. Some were left empty, some had plants or chemicals in and one had a small water wall set up in it, running with no water splashing beyond the tank.

The results show that with the right weather conditions, the tank with the moving water lost considerably more water than the still tanks and the presence of plants made little difference.

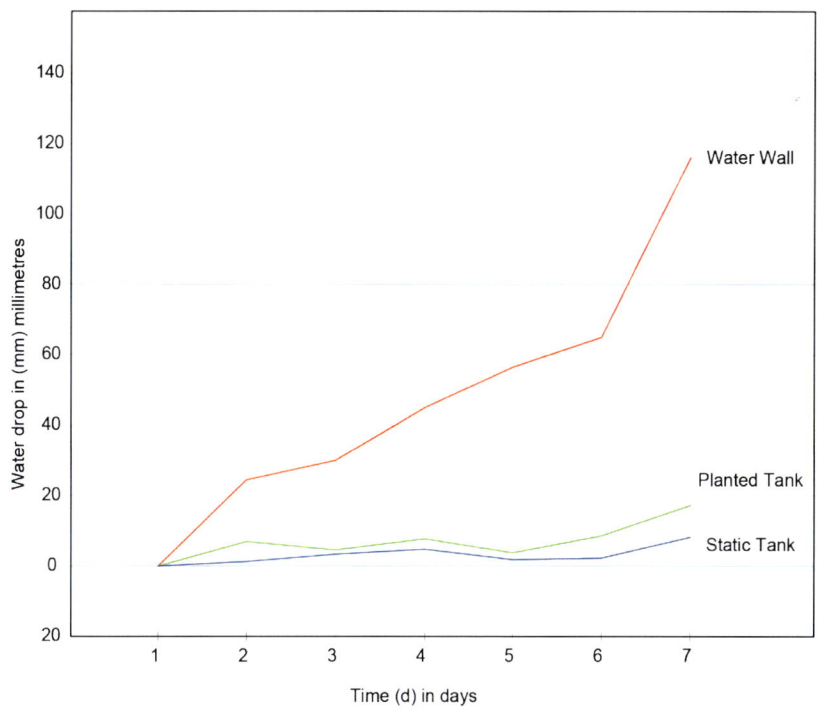

*Copper water chute under test.
Designer: Fairwater.*

Chutes

The most controllable method of dropping water from one level to another is to use an engineered chute. These smooth, gently rolled units, typically constructed from stainless steel or copper, will provide a clean sheet of water with minimal splashing. Although similar structures could be made from stone, they are difficult to roll and tend to have a coarser finish, which results in a more broken sheet of water.

In order to feed a chute, it is essential to provide a body of water behind. This could be an upper pool, or in the case of a wall chute, a back box is required. These are generally manufactured from polypropylene, and are connected to the delivery pipe from the pump. They allow the water, being delivered under pressure, to calm down and well up before spreading across the chute.

Multiple chutes were employed on the formal feature near Hatfield (above). To ensure the flow was maintained downstream, the combined widths of the chutes was maintained throughout, starting with one 3m-wide chute and ending with five of 600mm width.

The shape of the water as it falls is a factor of the speed it is flowing. The water will always gather into a plume, giving a triangular effect, but the faster the water flows, the more parallel the sheet sides will remain.

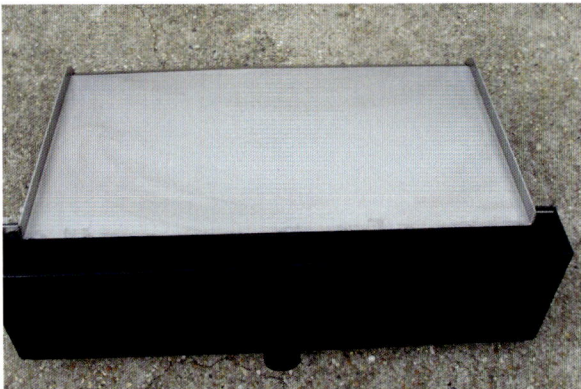

Chute with back box. Photo: Fairwater.

Multiple chutes in steel and granite. Designer: The Garden Company.

Errors – an example

Here is a Moorish garden I came across while on holiday in Malaysia many years ago. This is an elaborately-tiled structure with a water-bell fountain attachment. But it seemed to be short of water in the lower pond and was making a rather unpleasant sound.

On closer inspection I found the source of the noise: this submersible pump, in full view, was drawing air as it struggled to find sufficient water to operate the fountain. What a shame that this beautiful piece of work was ruined by the lack of an automatic top-up and nowhere discreet to house its workings!

Summary

Much of water garden construction is the art of concealment. Pumps, pipes, cables, filters and liners are all essential elements of a successful pool or pond, but all are unsightly. When installed without care and thought, the workings of the water garden can easily detract from the elegance of the design and the quality of the workmanship.

PART 2 INFORMAL WATER GARDENS

I like to think of informal water gardens as 'mimicking nature'. They are therefore much more concerned with re-creating naturally occurring pools, lakes, streams and waterfalls. My advice to anyone aspiring to create a natural-looking water garden is to spend some time considering them in the wild. Areas of the UK, such as the Welsh mountains, the Lake District or Yorkshire Moors, will inspire designers and their clients on the way water courses form, how rocks occur in the hillside and the way water behaves in its natural environment.

The place for informality in the garden

A pond or lake can provide a useful transition between the formality of the house and surrounding gardens and the informality of the landscape. The picture below shows a pond with a manicured formal lawn meeting the water's edge. But as the pond draws away from the house it becomes wilder and more informal.

The idea is that this is a naturally occurring body of water that preceded the building of the house. The lawn has been formalized on the house side by the introduction of a low brick wall beneath the

Semi-formal pond, Berkshire. Photo: Fairwater.

An informal pond, Norfolk. Designer: Julie Toll.

Informal lake. Designer: Fiona Lawrenson.

turf, but has been left in its natural state as it leads into the parkland.

A totally informal pond or lake, such as in the lower-left picture opposite, should satisfy a few simple criteria if it is to appear uncontrived and to have always existed.

Ponds and lakes generally form in valleys where water would have collected over many years, rarely on or half way up hills. With this in mind it is important to consider the topography of the site and to try and place the pond or lake in a hollow. The approach to the pond should at least be level, never rising.

There will be times when this is not possible and some excavated spoil will have to be used to create bunds and dams to retain the water, and provide a level rim to the pool. If this is the case, planting and subtle, rather than sudden, grades can be employed to disguise the adjustment in ground levels.

Excavation

Any pond or lake will require excavation works or even lowering ('reduce-dig') the ground level to accommodate paving or other landscaping elements.

The by-product of such excavation is a surplus of spoil, and the disposal of this material is a key cost-factor in the construction process of a pond or lake. Carting large quantities of material from site in lorries or skips is both expensive and environmentally harmful; it should be avoided where possible and the spoil considered as an asset. Surplus spoil can be spread as a thin film over a wide area of ground, such as an adjacent paddock, or used in ground-sculpting to create amphitheatres or gentle mounding. Some spoil may be required to adjust the ground levels and achieve a level working platform before the lake itself is excavated. A small amount will be needed to create marginal planting beds on completion.

Excavation for a lake in sand.

Finished lake. Both photos: Fairwater. Designer: Anthony Paul

The top left-hand picture shows a lake being excavated in sand. I would draw your attention to the level ledge cut around the perimeter, which is to accommodate the edge materials and ensure that any lining material is hidden from view.

In the lower left-hand picture large sandstone boulders were placed onto the ledge, on top of the lining to create the rock retaining wall.

One final point to emphasize about excavations is that soil in the ground will have compacted over years. When it is dug, it will loosen and take up more space. One cubic metre of sand in the ground will bulk by around 20 per cent so giving 1.2m3 to be disposed of. For clay soils this will increase to 30 per cent.

Definition of lakes and ponds

The English language has many words to describe both still and moving water, from loch, bourne, stream, canal to rill. The two most commonly-used words to describe still pools are lake and pond. It is worth understanding the difference between the two. Although other descriptions exist, my preferred definition of a lake is as an area of inland fresh water whose surface area is sufficient in size to be affected by wind action that results in waves, which in turn result in erosion. In other words, if the banks of the lake are being washed away over time, it is fair to refer to the body of water as a lake. The waves on this lake are clearly visible (right), and the potential erosion has been reduced by dense reed-bed planting around the margins.

Golf-course lake, Sussex. Photo: Fairwater.

There are occasions when spoil excavated from the pond or lake cannot be retained on site. An example would be when working on the flood plain of a river. The area of land adjacent to main rivers in the UK is given flood-plain status by the Environment Agency, the government body responsible for maintaining waterways. The land within this area is defined by a specific contour or ground height and cannot be raised in any way: to do so would reduce the space available for the river to spread into when it floods. If the river cannot spread into its flood plain, the surplus water will continue downstream and threaten conurbations.

This lake (right) was constructed on the flood plain of the river Thames near Henley and the excavated spoil, some 2000m^3 had to be transported in lorries, 15m^3 at a time, to a licensed tip.

*Lined lake.
Designer: Martin Lane-Fox.*

Liners for lakes or ponds

To be successful a pond or lake must obviously retain water. Levels will fluctuate with summer evaporation and winter rain but the excavation must be lined in a water-retentive material. Let us consider the various types of Lining:

- Clay,
- Bentonite/Volclay,
- Concrete,
- GRP/fibreglass.

Flexible sheet liners:
- Butyl/rubber,
- Plastic-based liners.

Clay

Historically clay was used when it was the only material available, but it can be damaged by external forces such as tree roots and burrowing animals. But more importantly, to stand a chance of retaining water, it has to be spread in a layer no less than 450mm and kept permanently wet to prevent it shrinking and cracking. If clay is the existing substrate on site and there is a permanent source of water available, not including the mains water supply, to keep the pond topped up during the summer months, then clay may be worth using. If the clay has to be imported, however, it means that the pond will have to be first over-dug by 450mm to accommodate the clay which itself will have to be carted in lorries, dressed into the excavation, compacted and kept moist by spraying water over it as the pond fills. This is an expensive process which will result in a sub-standard lining.

Further problems resulting from a clay lining include the fact that clay is both a very fine substrate and growing medium for aquatic plants. The former means that bottom-feeding fish such as carp will stir the clay particles into suspension. This will result in turbid or cloudy water which never settles out. In the latter case, clay will allow invasive plant species, such as *Typha latifolia* or *Phragmities australis* to rapidly colonize the pond. An inert lining will mitigate both of these risks.

Bentonite

Bentonite or Volclay are volcanic clays which expand to around 12 times their original size when in contact with water. These materials are supplied as sheets with the clay sandwiched between two layers of geo-textile felt.

Panels of 'bentomat' are then placed on the prepared excavation and overlapped to provide the waterproof layer.

Costs are comparable with good quality rubber or PVC sheet liners, but are about five times the weight, thereby making them relatively expensive to install as large plant is needed to cart and place the materials. The

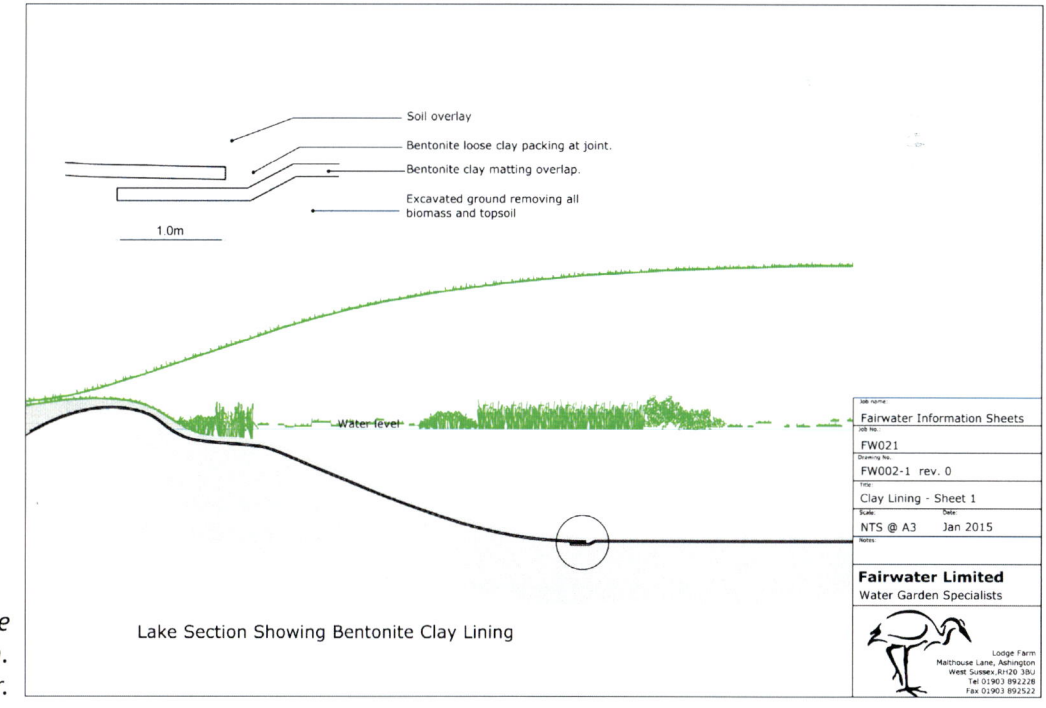

Bentonite installation. Fairwater.

Lake Section Showing Bentonite Clay Lining

main advantage of this material is that it will self-repair if penetrated.

Concrete

Reinforced concrete was used extensively by the Victorians as a lining to municipal lakes and ponds. It was often laid 450mm thick, but it had a limited life span and its cost would be prohibitive in anything but small pools today.

Concrete by itself is not a waterproof material; it has to have waterproofing additives mixed with it, and care has to be taken when laying it to ensure it is not contaminated or left with air bubbles in it. It is a non-flexible material so will crack with ground movements, and therefore has to be applied to a reinforcing mesh framework of steel to hold it together. It is much used in the swimming-pool construction business, where it often sprayed onto the steel mesh.

Modern concrete pools are extremely strong and durable, and much less likely to shrink and crack in the way that the Victorian pools did. The process is expensive, however, and best suited to high-quality swimming pools or Koi fish ponds. Exposed concrete surfaces will leech lime into the pond water, which in turn will produce a white precipitate and raise the pH; both can be combated in a pool by adjusting the water chemistry, though this is less of an option in biologically balanced ponds.

Fibreglass

Glass Reinforced Plastic (GRP) or Fibreglass are tough, durable waterproofing materials and well suited to lining concrete structures, formal ponds and so on. At eight or nine times the cost of installing flexible sheet liners, though, they do not provide a cost-effective method of waterproofing a large body of water.

Flexible sheet materials

There are two types: **PVC** or **Plastic-based liners** and **Rubber-based materials**. The better-quality products in either category will serve well and will typically come with a manufacturer's guarantee of around 20 years.

Prices will range from as low as £2.00 or £3.00 per square metre for a low-specification PVC up to £6.00 or £7.00 per square metre for the heavy-duty rubbers. It is down to personal preference which liner is chosen but in fact I favour the rubber ones for their elasticity.

Sprayed concrete being applied to form a pool shell. Photo: Guncast Pools.

Fibreglass-lined formal pond. Designer: Anthony Paul.

Lining a golf-course lake in 0.75mm butyl rubber. Photo: Fairwater.

Handling the 0.75mm butyl rubber lining for a golf-course lake. Photo: Fairwater.

Butyl and **EPDM** ('**Ethylene Propylene Diene Monomer**') rubbers are both man-made neoprene and by-products of the petrochemical industry. They have very good resistance to UV light and are some 200 per cent elastic, which makes them ideal to wrap behind walls, rocks and so on during pond construction. All these materials can be site-jointed with tapes or by specialist welding machinery, but the plastic-based liners do tend to be less flexible.

Butyl or **Greenseal EPDM** rubber pond liners are welded together in factories up to panel sizes of around 40m by 30m. This makes site installation relatively fast as other liners are generally supplied to site in rolls of up to 15m wide, meaning that more site-jointing is required.

The rolls, weighing about 1.2 metric tonnes are rolled out on top of a geo-textile underlay. They are then spread by hand, and then welded together to form a continuous sheet.

Smaller ponds up to 1200m^2 can be lined in a single sheet without the need for site welding.

Site-welding butyl liners. Photo: Fairwater.

Below-liner drainage. Photo: Fairwater.

LINERS FOR LAKES AND PONDS

Beneath the liner

Excavations in any type of ground will at some time retain water, whether or not it is lined. After heavy rain, water will gather beneath a pond liner for a period of time: the heavier the substrate, the longer the water will stay. So a predominately clay soil will hold water for several days, whereas a sand or shale soil will only retain water for a matter of hours.

If this water below the liner is not given an alternative route, it will take the path of least resistance and push against the pond liner above because the water on top of the liner is lighter than the soil beneath. As a result, the liner will float or bubble up, potentially causing serious damage.

It is therefore important to install a land drain beneath every pond liner; for example, a shallow trench backfilled with a 110mm perforated pipe and washed marine 20mm shingle. Failure to give the ground water passage can result in the phenomenon we refer to as 'Hippoing', as the bubbles of floating liner resemble basking hippos. It is difficult to deal with in a full lake or pond, so it really is a case where prevention is better than cure.

When organic material, such as silt, vegetation, soils, roots and so on are covered

A 'hippo' or floating liner. Photo: Fairwater.

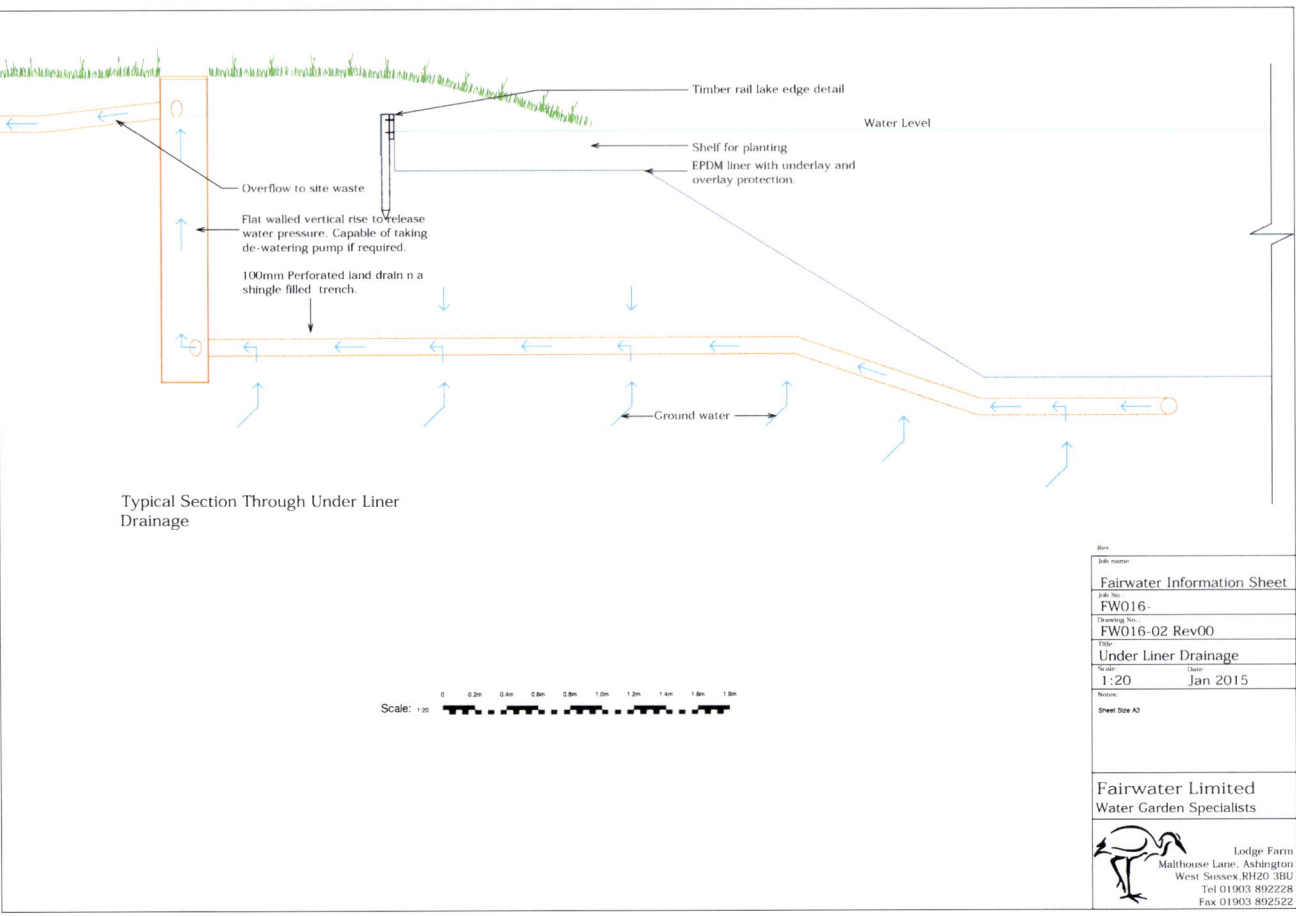

Section through a groundwater 'vent' arrangement. Plan: Fairwater.

by pond liners, a process of anaerobic decay will rapidly begin. The by-product of this decay is methane gas which will also gather beneath the liner and rise through the water taking the liner with it in a taught balloon. These bubbles, or gaseous 'hippos', are very difficult to deal with after the event and are again best prevented by ensuring the substrate beneath is carefully cleared of all organic material before the liner is laid.

It is not always possible to install a drain beneath a liner that is able to run downhill through the pond wall to a drainage ditch or soakaway. The pond or lake is often already in the lowest part of the site and the nearest ditch or drain is unlikely to be at a convenient 2m invert.

In these conditions a vertical pipe is installed at the end of the land drain. The weight of water on top of the liner means that the path of least resistance for the ground water is now up the smooth walled pipe rather than to displace the pond liner. An outlet pipe is taken from the vertical shaft at a convenient level for the site's surface-water drainage.

This vertical pipe is typically 300mm in diameter, which is wide enough to allow a submersible pump to be installed should the process described above need some mechanical assistance; perhaps because the lake is half full during initial filling or some maintenance works.

The fringes of ponds or lakes

Edges

After the pond has been excavated and lined, all the remaining work is around the margins. It is essential that the pond rim is set level so the water sits comfortably within its surroundings. It is also of paramount importance that the liner is hidden from view and protected from damage in this most vulnerable of areas.

If a formal lawn is to be brought to the water's edge, the detail of the grass meeting the pond must ensure that there is no boggy, soft strip of grass which cannot be mowed.

The detail securing the liner must be robust if the pond is to be planted and the liner held at the correct level and protected from the gardener's maintenance activities. My favoured technique for forming these two edging details is to use a concrete block on the formation ledge.

Soft edge / Hard edge

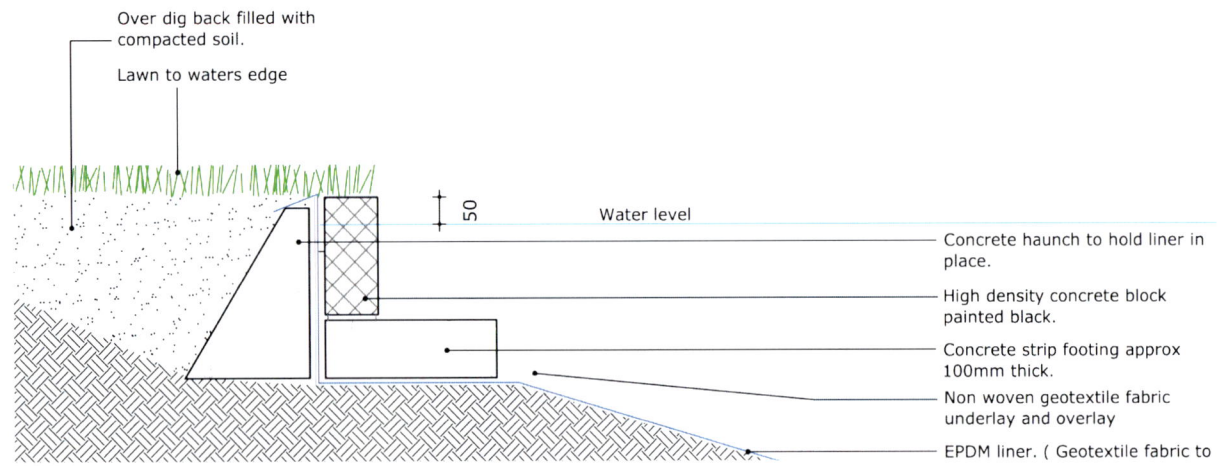
Detail of pond edge. Fairwater.

Marginal planting

In cases where an emergent margin is required to create a wildlife-friendly edge to the pond, suitable for planting, the 300mm-deep ledge is extended to at least 1500mm wide.

The block edge is then installed as described above, but excavated soils are dressed over the liner at a grade of about 1:5 to form a gentle slope into the water. Most of this overlaid soil should be the inert subsoil

The ledge will be cut during excavation, typically 300mm below water level. The excavation is first lined with geo-textile underlay and then the Greenseal or other sheet liner. A second layer of geo-textile protects the liner from above, just to the front of the ledge, and a concrete footing is poured approximately 100mm high. The concrete block is then laid free-hand to define the shape of the pond, and set level by a site level or long spirit level. Once laid, the liners are brought up behind the block edge and held in place with a concrete haunch before being trimmed level with the top of the block edge.

Because the block is laid within the liner, it will be sitting in the water and will thus become saturated. As a result it is possible to lay turf directly onto the block without the need for soil, and the dry lawn is therefore taken right to the water's edge.

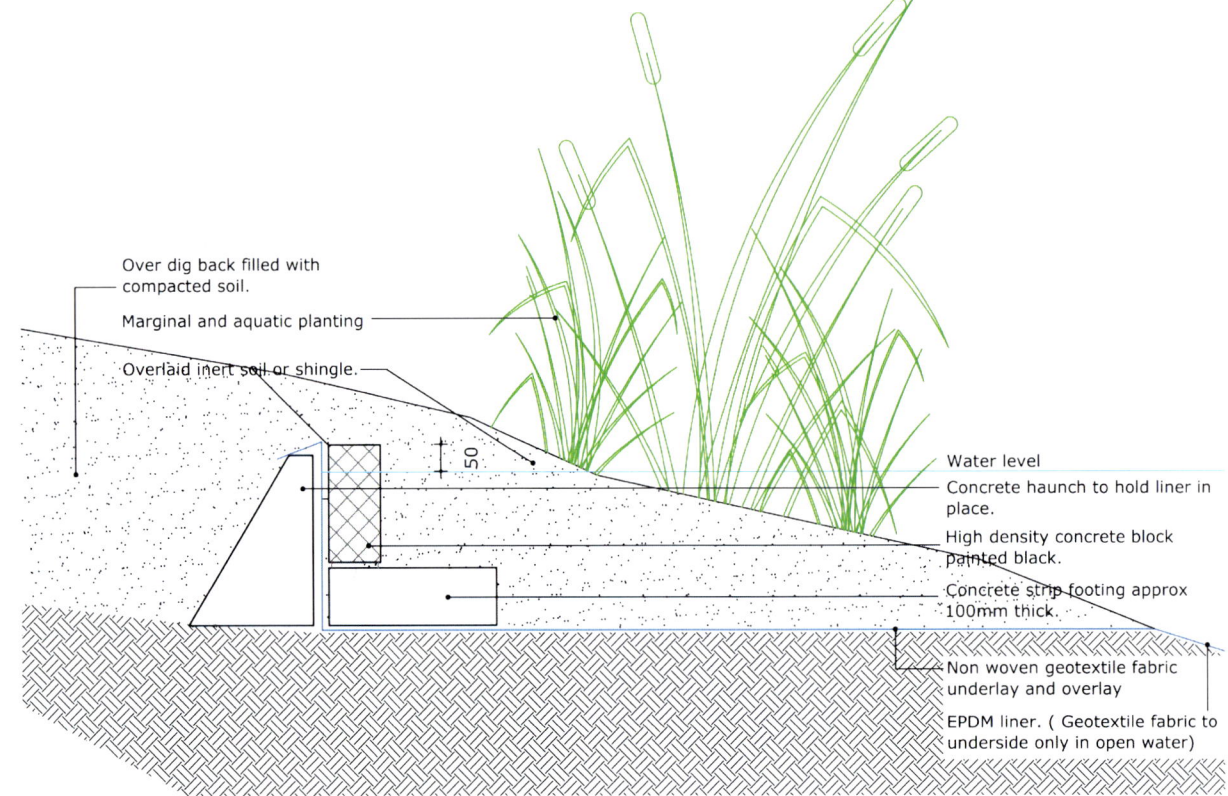
Detail of pond edge and planting. Fairwater.

from the excavation rather than rich topsoil. It is needed to provide anchorage for the plants, not to provide them with nutrients. The pond water will have plenty of the phosphates, nitrates and so on that plants need to grow, and the more of these water-borne nutrients they utilize, the fewer will be left available for the dreaded algae to grow on.

Wherever possible, my advice is that marginal plants are given a wet bed such as this to grow in, rather than placed in baskets on a shelf.

A lake edge. Designer: Fiona Lawrenson.

This picture shows the emergent edge being constructed. In the distance the block edge is being laid and in the foreground the position of the block wall can be seen. The margin has been overlaid predominantly with excavated yellow, sandy subsoil and has been dressed over with topsoil for aesthetic purposes.

Confining the overlaid soils to the margin in this way will help limit the spread of invasive marginal plant species.

Water plants

Water lilies (*Nymphaea*) can be planted on to the liner by preparing them with a little clay soil wrapped up in a hessian bag rather than a pot. The bag of soil and lily crown can be placed on the liner once the lake is full. When the hessian breaks down over the next couple of years, the lily will put out roots into the silt.

Clay-lined ponds

The vast majority of my work is with rubber-lined lakes and ponds, as site conditions rarely exist to enable the formation of a clay-lined pond. To remind you of my criteria: the clay must be already on site as the indigenous sub-soil, and there must be an available source of water to ensure that the water level does not drop and thus allow the clay to dry out.

If we do find a small stream on a clay site and are able to get permission from the relevant authorities to build a pond, a clay core dam will be required. The course of the stream is most likely to be sloping, so the site of the pond will need to be levelled; typically by a process of cut and fill whereby the upstream slopes are steepened to the proposed water level, and the downstream end is lifted or filled to create a dam.

The dam will have a core of the best clay on the site which will be compacted in layers of 100 to 200mm as a wall starting in a trench cut well into the virgin ground. While the dam is constructed, clay is added at a minimum 1:5 slope to the upstream side. This gentle slope will reinforce the dam and is less likely to suffer damage from erosion over time.

The running water from the stream is given a secondary outfall around the dam to ensure it does not wash the structure away when the stream is in spate. A solid structure, such as a rock wall, can be added to take a measured flow of water over the dam if required.

Permission for this type of pond is becoming increasingly difficult to obtain. The Environment Agency is concerned that damming even small streams will affect the delicate silting process along the whole length of the water course, and will prevent fish migrating upstream to breed.

Off-line ponds may stand a better chance of being granted permission when the pond is built alongside the stream rather than across it, and a controlled, pipe feed is taken from the stream to fill the pond as required.

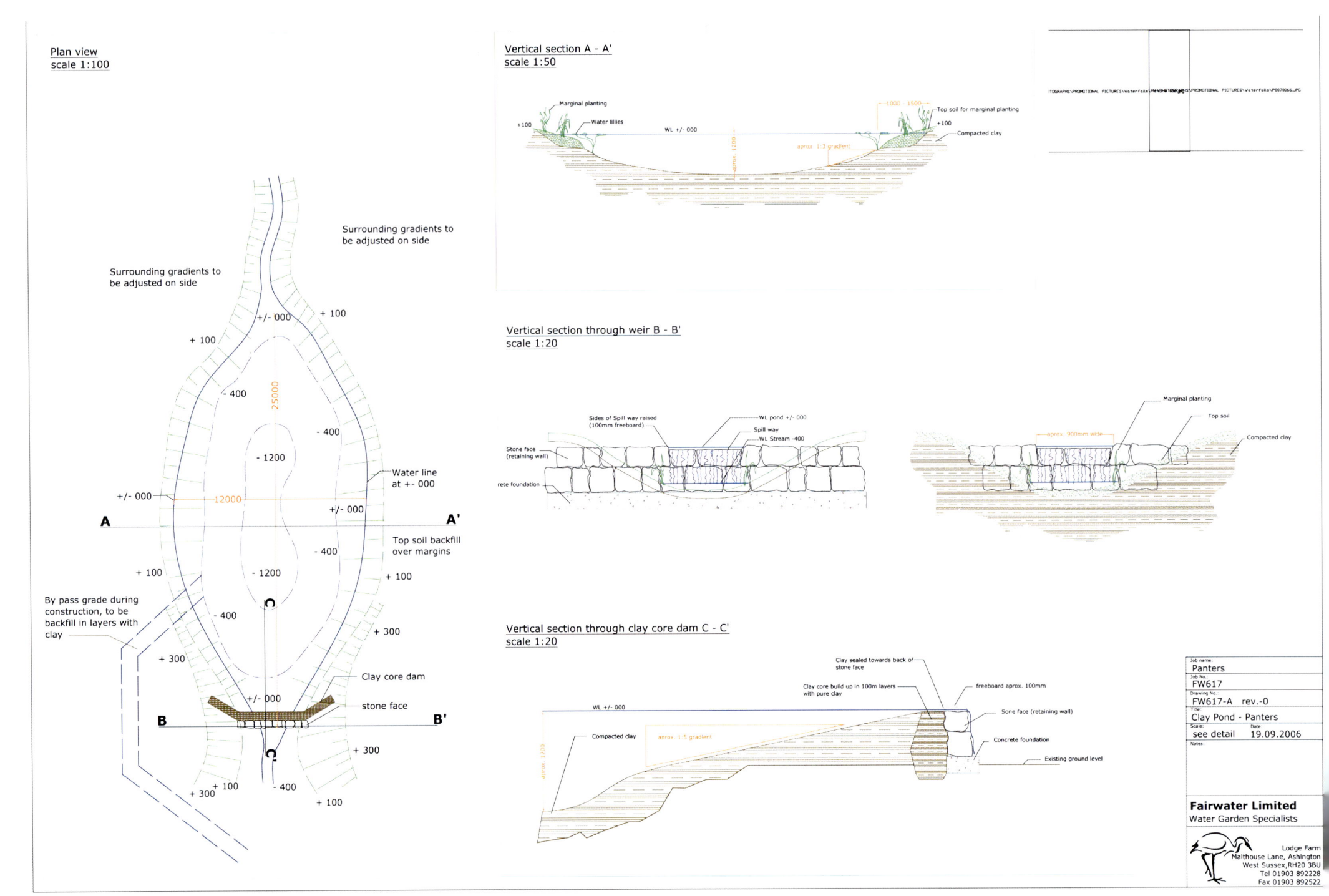

Details of a clay-lined pond construction.

34 INFORMAL WATER GARDENS

CASE STUDY — Extending a clay-lined pond

Let us now follow a case study of a project in East Sussex. This existing clay-lined farm pond was to be extended as shown by the white flags. The meadow beyond was planted with wild flowers and orchids, so the spoil was to be retained close to the pond to be sculpted on completion.

Owing to the fact that this was drained farm land, we were unable to guarantee that there would be no old land drains or other drainage layers in the extended area. The client was therefore given a choice: we could try to complete the works without artificial lining but, if the pond failed to hold water, it was at his risk and the liner could always be added in the future; to guarantee a finished water level would require us to fit a liner. He chose the latter solution as he did not relish the idea of revisiting the works a year or two later.

Although constructing or altering a garden pond is technically an engineering operation, it will not necessarily require planning permission. The specific rules vary between authorities but generally garden ponds and water features can be built under 'permitted development rights'. A pond or lake in a paddock beyond the curtilage of the house will require planning permission because to construct it will usually be changing the use of the land, typically from agricultural to parkland.

Construction work

This picture shows the project progressing and the water and organic materials being removed to the spoil heap ready for lining works.

The excavation for the extension to the lake is under way and the formation ledge is clearly visible. The yellow excavator is starting to dig the trenches for the under-liner drainage pipes, and rolls of geo-textile underlay can be seen in the foreground.

To reduce costs, a timber rail will be used to maintain the liner at the required height on this project in place of the concrete block wall described earlier. This method does not give the option of lawn to the water's edge but it does provide a level and precise structure which will ensure the liner is held at the required level before being overlaid.

The diagram on the next page shows the timber rail, a 25mm by 150mm board screwed to the vertical 50mm by 50mm posts. The timber is a pressure-treated soft wood which

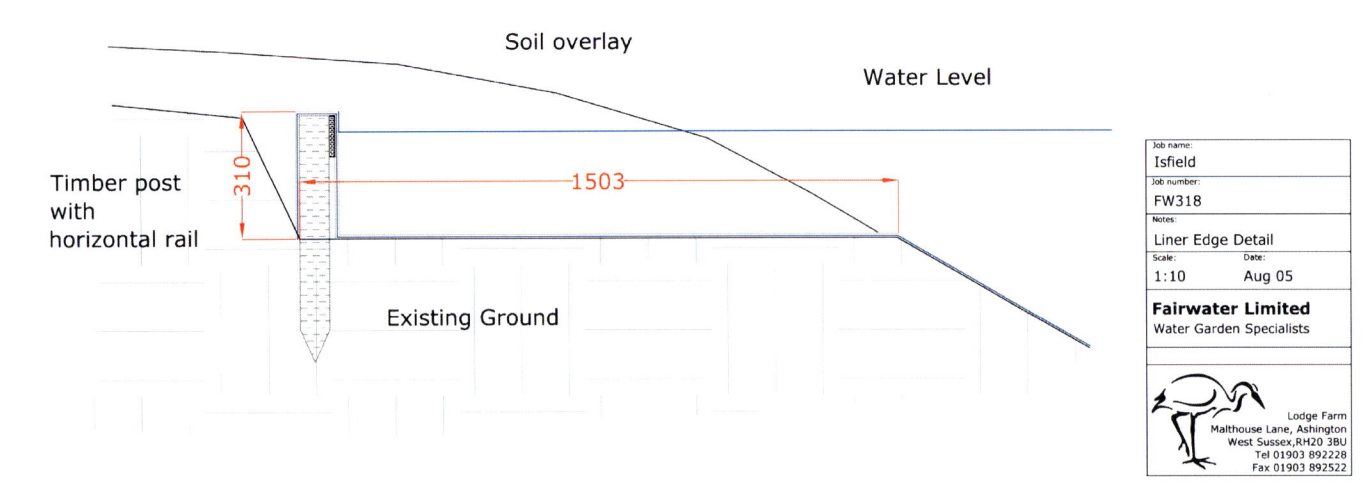

Detail of timber rail. Fairwater.

should last for 15 years in the ground, by which time the liner will be secure with the soil overlay and root masses of the plants quite stable.

The two pipes on the left of the picture show that the land drain and the vertical shaft from beneath the liner are in place ready to deal with any ground water.

There is a balancing tank next to these pipes as now the lake is to be fitted with a rubber liner. It is possible to install an automated top-up to maintain the water level over the summer months.

The EPDM Greenseal liner has been rolled out ready for unfolding into a sheet.

The precisely level edge provided by the timber rail is evident, and the wide ledge is being protected from above by a surcharge of geo-textile underlay.

At the far end a concrete slab has been poured to accommodate stepping stones; any structures such as bridges, jetties, decks, islands and so on, are built up from concrete footings poured on top of the liners.

Newly planted with *Butomus umbellatus*, the flowering rush, the lake has been full for a couple of months. The spoil has been shaped into a deliberate hill with a 'double helix' path providing access up and back down.

The lake has now been extended and lined in the grey geo-textile.

The lake starts to fill as all the work is now at the margin.

36   INFORMAL WATER GARDENS

Two years later, the lake and its planting have matured.

Bill of Quantities

Job: Clay Lake Extension
Designed by Nigel Philips
January 2015
All figures are subject to the addition of VAT

Code	Description	Quantity	Unit	Rate	Total
A	TECHNICAL DESIGN Sum to prepare detailed technical drawings and specifications	1.00	sum	1,600.00	1,600.00
B	DRAIN EXISTING POND Erect temporary tank, net and air pump to accommodate fish during works, transfer fish	1.00	sum	1,190.00	1,190.00
C	PREPARATION Strip topsoil from area to receive spoil Place in weathered bunds on site	1.00	sum	1,896.00	1,896.00
D	EXISTING TREE ROOT Excavate tree root and cart from site	1.00	sum	1,264.75	1,264.75
E	DREDGE POND Dredge pond of all silt and organic material not required for future use Cart silt locally and spread as thin as possible	1.00	sum	4,272.00	4,272.00
F	EXTEND POND Excavate to extend pond as shown on drawing no. 335	1.00	sum	4,320.00	4,320.00
G	UNDERLINER DRAINAGE 110mm perforated pipe in 20mm bed and surround Access shaft and connection to ditch	1.00	sum	2,105.50	2,105.50
H	LINER Supply and fit 0.75mm SealEco EPDM pond liner on 250g/m2 geotextile underlay	1.00	sum	12,329.81	12,329.81
I	BALANCING TANK For primary overflow and top up	1.00	sum	3,105.00	3,105.00
J	TIMBER RAIL To support liner at back of ledge	1.00	sum	2,240.00	2,240.00
K	OVERLAY LINERS Place excavated soils on to liners to form marginal planting beds	1.00	sum	1,890.00	1,890.00
L	LANDSCAPE SPOIL Shape spoil heap and compact ready for landscaping	1.00	sum	3,000.00	3,000.00
M	TOPSOIL Spread topsoil and leave ready for cultivation and planting by others	1.00	sum	2,184.00	2,184.00
N	BOARD WALK & JETTY 150x150mm sawn green oak uprights 150x50mm sawn green oak framework 150x30mm sawn green oak deck boards	1.00	sum	9,942.00	9,942.00
O	MARGINAL & AQUATIC PLANTING Supply and plant 3000 x 1Litre plants	1.00	sum	10,080.00	10,080.00
	TOTAL				**£61,419.06**

CASE STUDY — CLAY-LINED POND

All rockery stone has a 'grain'. Designer: Rose Leonard.

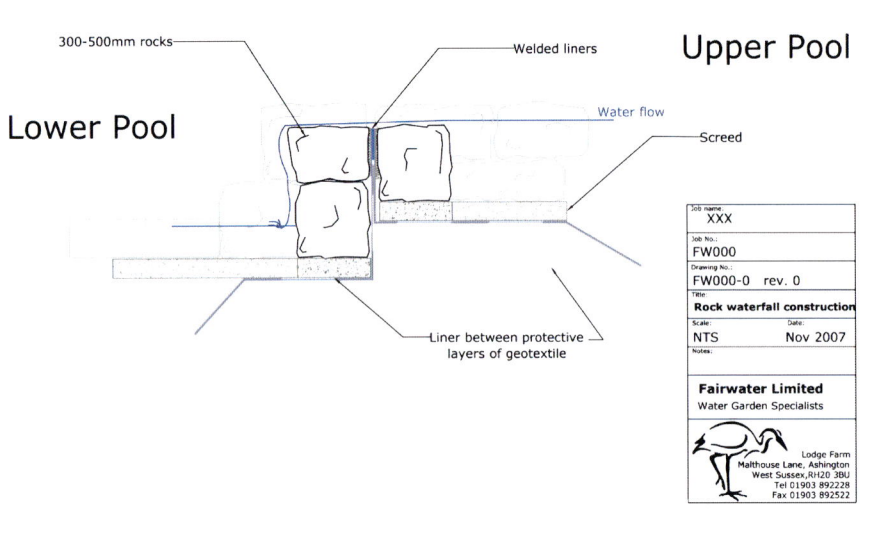

Typical section through a constructed waterfall. Plan: Fairwater.

Natural water courses

Earlier I suggested that re-creating natural water courses was best attempted after studying the way they behave in their natural setting and this could not be truer than when looking at natural stone waterfalls.

From my own observations, I have a few basic rules about how rocks should be placed if they are to look natural.

First, the water flowing down a hillside would have washed away loose soils leaving the hard rock. The water is therefore flowing perpendicular to the rocks. The rock-face extends beyond the immediate channel of water, so it is important to form outcrops beyond the water course as if they have been exposed when the stream was running particularly fast one winter.

Second, all rock has a grain which should be set to run in the same direction; level is the easiest. This grain shows how the rock was formed in the quarry; it should go back into the ground as it came out.

Third, when placing rocks, the best effect will be gained from using the largest rocks that are physically possible to move. They will still be blocks of stone, and it should be remembered that it is not a brick wall that is being built; vertical joints should be set to continue as if they are fissures rather than joint bridges as in stretcher bond brickwork.

A water course could be built as a cascade of rock or as a series of level pools. I prefer the latter, as there will always be a time when the pump is switched off and, as with pools, the water course will always retain some water and therefore interest. As a cascade it will look sad without the water running over it.

Sheet liners are used between columns of rock to form the rock pools with the liners from each pool carefully joined and concealed between the rocks forming the spillway.

All rocks are set in concrete to ensure they will not fall over, and the liners are generally concreted over to protect them.

Topography

It is important to work with the lie of the land if a waterfall or stream is to look authentic. On occasions, however, usually because there is a requirement to view the falling water from a particular position, the waterfall has to be built against the topography of the site.

In this example limestone blocks have been laid at an angle to give the impression that the whole structure was a result of a 'heave' in the ground. Designer: John Murdoch.

The viewer may or may not be convinced by attempts at producing a geological phenomenon. Perhaps the tree ferns and olive trees do give an incongruous Mediterranean feel to this part of semi-rural Hertfordshire! The effect of the 2m-high waterfall is nonetheless striking. Designer: John Murdoch.

Waterfalls and streams

Building waterfalls and streams is extremely subjective. It is impossible to draw the feature in detail. So much will depend on how the delivered rock is put together by the individual doing the building on the day.

Mock-up of a stream flowing through rocks. Photo: Fairwater.

This example of a stream in Leicestershire was the subject of a heated debate between designer, client and contractor. No-one could clearly convey their ideas to the others by drawing alone. It was suggested that everyone chose or took pictures of waterfalls they had seen and liked. The picture above actually consists of up to six different sites stitched together, based on a shot of the specific site. Once everyone was happy, this picture was used in place of a plan.

The finished waterfall, constructed from large pieces of York block stone was true to the picture and all parties were happy. Designer: Julie Toll.

Types of stone

Where possible, a local stone should be used to make a waterfall look authentic. In the south of England, for example, sandstones and limestone are prevalent, although many areas are of clay or chalk which tend not to contain significant quantities of rock. Sand or limestone will weather to a dull grey in time and as such will tend to blend in. However, moving inappropriate rock from miles away will never result in a natural look.

Welsh granite has been carted to an urban Surrey garden and, although the rock-laying principles have been followed, the result will always appear contrived. Photo: Fairwater.

Sussex sandstone waterfall. Photo: Fairwater.

Construction of a water course in Kent. Photos: Fairwater. Designers: Acres Wild.

Construction

In this photo of construction of a water course shows the limestone being laid across the path of the water. It can be seen taking the place of the block edge on the far side of the picture where it is sitting on a blackened concrete footing on top of the liners.

A stepped Japanese bridge (above) is under construction here, built up on a raft poured on top of the liners. The marginal planting beds are being filled with on-site soils.

At the head of the water course is a fissure in the rock. The delivery pipe from the pump at the bottom of the valley can be seen on the right of the picture.

In the same way, a steel water-chute needs a back box to take the sting out of the water being delivered under considerable pressure from the pump. So a waterfall benefits from a sump behind the weir which is filled by the pump and overflows over the waterfall.

The maturing pond

Any body of water, be it a lake, pond, formal or informal pool, will require maintenance to keep it as a pond. From the first day of filling, the pond is being changed by a natural process called silting.

Left to its own devices over a period of years or decades, a pond will fill with silt. Soils and rotting vegetation are washed or blown into the pool where they settle to the floor and break down.

Gradually, as more and more silt is added, the water level in the pool reduces and the soils are colonized with ever higher plant species that dry them out. Eventually soil conditions will allow tree saplings to colonize, and the pool will have reached its climax community. Termed a 'hydrosere', this process is unavoidable, and can only be stemmed by the periodic removal of the silt from the water. This process is called dredging, and may be done annually by hand in a small pond, or mechanically every few decades for a large lake.

As the silt decays, it uses oxygen and produces carbon dioxide as a waste product. Plants use the carbon dioxide as they grow and produce oxygen as their waste product. This is a very simple description of the basic gas cycle in a pond. In actual fact, it is much more complex and other gases are involved. However, a stagnant pond is one where the oxygen in the water is less than the carbon dioxide. The higher forms of life — insects and fish — will die once the oxygen levels fall, and the addition of air pumps and fountain aerators will only delay the process.

A maturing pond. Photo: Landmark.

Chiddingfold village pond, West Sussex. Photo: Fairwater.

Summary

A naturally balanced pond or lake will look after itself provided it is well planted and is not artificially fed with nutrients, be they fish food, fertilizers or excessive quantities of silt. The pond will sustain a balanced weight of fish within its delicate ecosystem, but as soon as these fish are fed or artificially protected from external predators, this intricate balance will be upset and the pond will have too many fish and a surplus of nutrients. These nutrients will be used by the airborne algae spores to colonize the pond and turn it green. In time, the more complex filamentous algae, commonly referred to as blanket weed, may colonize. It is only when the pond ecosystem has been interfered with that the addition of filtration equipment is required.

Further reading

Archer-Wills, A. (2000) *The Water Gardener*. (paperback) Frances Lincoln, London.

Brooks, A. & Agate, E. (1976, rev. ed. 2001) *Waterways and Wetlands*. BTCV, Doncaster.

Hopwood, R. (2009) *Fountains & Water Features — From Ancient Springs to Modern Marvels*. Frances Lincoln, London.

Littlewood, M. (2001) *Landscape Detailing 4 - Water*. Routledge, Abingdon.

Littlewood, M. (2008) *Natural Swimming Pools — A Guide for Building*. Agrimedia, London.

Littlewood, M. (2013) *Natural Swimming Pools — Conventional Pool Conversion Guide*. Rev. ed. Ecodesignscape, Hinton St George.

Index

algae 6, 7, 8, 9, 10, 33, 47

baffling 9
balancing tanks 6, 9, 10, 11, 12
   dimensions 6
   placement 6, 13
bentomat 27
bentonite 27
bills of quantities 6, 13, 39
blanket weed 8, 47
boulders iv
break gap 7
brimming pools 9, 11
bromine *see* chemicals
butyl 28, 29

canals 1, 8
   and *see* rills
chadar 20
chemicals 7, 8, 9, 11, 28
   bromine 7, 9
   chlorine 7
chutes 16, 19, 22, 43
cladding 9, 20
clay 25, 27, 33, 34
cobbles 8
concrete
   blocks 2
      edging 31-33
   liners 28
   shell 2, 3
coping 14
copper 9, 10, 22

cracking 1, 2, 28
cryptosporidium 7

dams
   clay-core 33, 34
dosing unit, chemical 6, 7, 9
drainage
   below-liner 29, 30, 31
drowning 17
dust 19

edging, edges of pools
   infinity 9
   knife 9, 10
   materials 25
   metal 9, 10
   ponds & lakes 31-34
Environment Agency 26, 33
ethylene propylene diene monomer (EPDM) 29
evaporation 21
excavation 25, 32
expansion joints 1
expense 4

fibre-glass 2, 3, 28
filtration 9, 10
flexible pond liners 2, 8, 28, 29
float valves 6
flood plain 26
flow rates 15, 16, 19, 22
footings 2, 43
formal ponds, pools 2
fountains 4
   rings 4

gap, break 7
gas, methane 30
geo-textile underlays 32
glass covering 7
glass reinforced plastic (GRP) 28
granite 20
gravel 10
greenseal EPDM liners 29
grilles 17
ground
   levels, sculpting 25
   water 30

'head', height of fall 15, 19, 20
header tanks 7
'hippo', floating liner 30
hydrosere 46

informal ponds, lakes 24-25
infinity edges 9, 10
Iris laevigata 10
irrigation tanks 45

jets
   costs 11
   fountains 1, 4, 5, 6
   jumping, laminar flow 11
joints, expansion 1

lakes iv, 24, 25, 26
land
   change of use 35
   drain 30
ledges, pond 32
levels, ground 25, 33